CATCH 36

Poems by Susie Cornfield

Illustrations by Sara Rapoport

Catch 36
Published by Garret Books Ltd, 2010
ISBN 978-0-9552279-5-0

Copyright © Susie Cornfield
www.susiecornfield.com

Illustrations © Sara Rapoport
www.sararapoport.com

The right of Susie Cornfield to be identified as the author of this work has been asserted in accordance with the Copyright, Designs and Patents Act 1988.

All rights reserved. No part of this publication may be reproduced, stored in or introduced into a retrieval system, or transmitted, in any form or by any means (electronic, mechanical, photocopying, recording or otherwise) without the prior written permission of both the copyright owner and the publisher of this book.

Garret Books Ltd, Company Registration Number: 5647052
Registered address: Suite 210 Maddison House, 226 High Street, Croydon CR9 1DF, Surrey, UK
www.garretbooks.com

A CIP catalogue record for this book is available from the British Library.

Designed and typeset by
Caroline and Roger Hillier, The Old Chapel Graphic Design
www.theoldchapellivinghoe.com

Copy editors: Ros Jesson and Isobel Rapoport

Printed and bound in the UK by
Cromwell Press Group, Trowbridge, Wiltshire BA14 0XB

Visit www.catch36.com

For

Alison, Victoria and Charlotte

Pat, Donna, Sara, Alma and Ted

&

Ian

Also by the author

Fiction
Green Fire, a satirical thriller, second in the series
The Chronicles of Dekaydence (Garret Books, 2009,
ISBN 978-0-9552279-3-6).
Black Light, a satirical thriller, first in the series
The Chronicles of Dekaydence (Garret Books, 2008,
ISBN 978-0-9552279-2-9), published originally as
The Sticky Rock Café.
Visit www.dekaydence.com

Non-fiction
Farewell, My Lovely, 2nd edition, a collection of tributes to
much-loved departed pets (Garret Books, 2009,
ISBN 978-0-9552279-4-3), a much-extended edition of the
original paperback *Farewell, My Lovely* (Garret Books, 2006,
ISBN 978-0-9552279-1-2).
Visit www.farewellmylovely.com

History
The Queen's Prize, the story of the National Rifle Association
of Great Britain (Pelham Books, 1987, ISBN 0-7207-1751-5).

Contents

LOSS   11
The Time Chasm   12
One of the Good People has Gone   14
Becalmed Within a Storm (*On the loss of a close friend*)   16
The Visitor   20
My Old Aunt has Died   24
A Beautiful Autumnal Day   28
Mimi   30
A Bientôt   32
A Hymn of Hope   35

NATURE   37
The Old Fox   38
The Gardener's Boat   41
Wishful Thinking   42
The New Bird in Town   44
Mr Turner, I Presume   47

LOVE   51
Help   52
Wedding Blossom   54
Lost Love   56
The Love Scavenger   58
In Recovery   60
For You   62
Wedding Frost   64
The Dance   65
The Ducks   67

FUN 69
Writer, Beware! 70
The Sales 72
SPAMutations 74
e-Invitation to a Dance 75
e-Call to a Friend 77

SPLEEN 79
Farewell to Alms 80
A Year on the Dole (in the 1990s) 82
Daylight Robbery 86

PLAY AREA 91
There are Monsters in My Room 92
I Want to Stay Up Late Tonight 99
Overture and Beginners 103
Baby Blues 108

HAPPY ENDING 115
The Face Rainbow 116

Information Area 120
Should you want to know more about a poem...

LOSS

The Time Chasm

A small table stands between but it is two hands that
 divide us.
A barrier of moons and sunrises, and sand
trickling through the glass, and back and forth across the
 beach.

You stand on the shore and watch as I sail towards you.
The boat staggers drunkenly, lurches and stumbles over
 the water.
You smile. Quietly. Gently.
I shall never match you as a sailor, I know, but you will
 never say.

From the shore you send a light, bright as a chandelier
 amid black velvet,
but a fog surrounds me.
I have swallowed too much grey mist.
I can not follow its direction.

The candles that I hold can never match that beam;
they flicker for a moment in the cloud,
gasping for life,
bow their flames in sorrow and expire.

LOSS

We sit at the table,
a cloth of white foam between,
winter and laughter, summer and tears,
our unfair fare.

The hands dividing us soften and bend—
for a brief moment
the furrows in the cloth are smoothed away.

When I reach the shore you will be gone.
You say you can not leave a footprint
as the sand does not feel your tread.

For once, I do not believe you.

I shall see your mark and
   follow it along the shore
until I see you wave
and then ...
two hands dividing us
will no more.

One of the
Good People has Gone

One of the good people has gone.
One of the steady people,
the kind, reliable, ready people
who don't take centre stage
or rant or rave
against the world
but just get on with it.

One of the good people has gone.
A quietly friendly, gently humorous man
who lived his life honourably and with principle,
who loved his wife,
adored his children,
and was kind to his mum and dad;
who cherished his family,
who relished his friends,
and an occasional curry.

One of the good people has gone.
Someone who didn't make the news,
who didn't win medals – excepting as a team player;
who was an organiser, behind the scenes,
helping others run their business,
helping others have fun and play the game.

Yes, he was one of the good people
who moves through life
causing but a ripple,
but, in leaving, creates
a tidal wave of loss and sadness.

One of the good people has gone
and those of us who are left
see now, more clearly than before,
that this good man stood out from so many of the rest.

Becalmed Within a Storm

On the loss of a close friend

An autumn sun shines benignly;
the trees shed tears of bronze, copper and gold,
as I walk into this ivory and gold nave,
the vaulted air scented with lilies.
I am one of several hundred
saying goodbye, bidding farewell.
I am among friends
But I stand alone, raw in emptiness, becalmed within a storm.

I was not brother, cousin, nephew or son
to this man who has died too young.
I am not seated in the places reserved for family,
I am not mentioned in memories, or in despatches.
I was a friend. Like many here. A good friend, I hope,
as he was to me.
I am among friends
but I stand alone, raw in emptiness, becalmed within a storm.

LOSS

I will not get a card, or tears of sympathy,
the thoughts of care, the supportive hug.
I've had no need of such, until this day.
And yet ...
My wife stands at my side and weeps.
She looks to me. For comfort? To offer support?
But I am in a desert,
tears do not come, the well of grief lies too deep, too
  worn.
The priest's words fall about me,
like bleached and hollow bones.
And I stand alone, raw in emptiness, becalmed within
  a storm.

I am torn, and confused, by the jagged wrench of loss.
Parts of me I never knew existed will no longer
  connect – or be,
and are now numb, blind, hopelessly searching
for the intangible wire, whatever it was this friend
  provided.

LOSS

I have lost a friend.
Someone with whom I shared a beer, a laugh,
a thought, a problem, a celebration,
in an unseen bond, dense, flexible, and indestructible.
Or so it seemed.
I was not brother, cousin, nephew or son,
I was a friend, a good friend.
And in this moment, and for many to come,
I shall stand alone, raw in emptiness, becalmed within a storm,
remembering, and missing, a good friend.

The Visitor

She'd never really noticed the visitor before.
He'd always been someone else's guest.

She'd been places after he'd left
and touched the sharp edge of his visiting card.
A chill had pierced her heart fleetingly
but left no scar.

Then one day she saw him at a distance,
recognising him as he passed,
and for a moment
she felt her senses freeze.

Suddenly, with no warning,
he was visiting her, forever calling out of the blue,
shedding grey shadows wherever he walked.

At first, she recognised him only as a shadow,
of someone she thought she knew.
A shadow flitting across the room
that made her catch her breath, no more.

But then he chose to stay, moving in,
gradually, stealthily,
casting fine cobwebs over everything that was hers.

She began by brushing them away, as she'd been taught,
but when they grew back, thicker than before,
she learnt, had to learn, to resist the struggle.

Still, she hoped to return and find him gone
but he was always there to greet her, though he never did.
He never spoke and she could never look him in the eye.

She thought the presence of friends,
the sound of their voices and laughter,
would drive him away.

But he was too wily for her and hid from their view.
And she saw him still. Hovering in the room beyond,
lingering on the stairs, waiting for her. Always waiting.
And he came to her only when they had gone.

He took to turning off the lights.
He put up a screen to block the
  sun from her soul
and the moon from her
  eyes.
She searched for
  light, any light,
but it became harder
  to find.
There was a
  candle ... but
  where was the
  match?

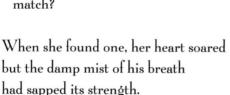

When she found one, her heart soared
but the damp mist of his breath
had sapped its strength.

Her blood turned to tears and through them
she felt her heart sink, as if through quicksand,
slowly, irretrievably,
down into her body, down and beyond.

She began to struggle for breath but only his came.
For the first time, she looked up and stared
straight into his face ...
She saw him, felt him, incline towards her.
He brought his mouth to hers
and wound his arms round her neck.
She felt her blood,
which'd turned to tears, turn now to ashes.

He was inflaming her, with a passion inflamed with ice,
and she knew then that she had been the visitor.
Only he had the right to belong.

When they called for her next morning,
in the bright light of day, they found her gone.

It was the boy living on the streets
who saw the visitor,
stared straight into his face and shuddered as he passed
  by.
It was the boy who picked up the grey calling card
and put it in his pocket.

My Old Aunt has Died

My old aunt has died.
Hard of hearing, physically frail, a bit crotchety,
but sharp as a jungle of monkeys.
And a mother, not through the usual channel,
but in her kindness and care
of her young brother,
her cats, her tortoises,
as well as my cousins, and me.

My old aunt has died,
taking with her a sackful of memories
and a boatload of the history of relatives
from foreign shores,
a foreign religion and culture,
of which I wish I'd captured more.
And of her best friend, her sister, my mother,
the dark-eyed ebony-hair'd deep one,
such a contrast to my lively, auburn hair'd, blue-eyed old
    aunt.

There had been a life of diamonds,
couture clothes, and chandeliers,
dinners of many courses, and wines,
and rooms overflowing with flowers.
An uncle with a ballroom and
a bellboy'd lift in his house.
An uncle who lived in the Georges V, Paris
and holiday'd in the golden days of Liverpool's Adelphi—
with special meals brought in.

A household of seven children,
playing and laughing,
with cousins, and friends.
And my unknown grandfather smiling,
apparently my smile,
never happier than when all his brood
were with him, under his roof.

But the time of two sisters riding,
carefree and bareback along the sandy beach,
and of dancing and parties,
turned to war, to deaths,
into a family disintegrating,
amidst blood and loss,
and seven candles.

I have one memory of my grandmother,
in a white nightdress,
standing by her bed assisted by two daughters.
An old woman, her hair falling to her waist,
free as the wind, dark as a raven's wing.
Eyes full of fear,
as she stares at me, a small child—
worried p'haps that I'm some wayward addition?

She'd lived for years behind an asylum's bars,
when suffering became too great to bear,
while other bars kept her from her husband's family.
What kind of god insists on this?
What kind of family carries out this "law"?
What kind of sorrows did she endure?
What sorrows did my old aunt,
my mother and their siblings know?
I'll never know for sure,

because

My old aunt has died.
And with her a sackful of memories.

LOSS

But I have a memory of my own,
more pungent than the scent of my old aunt's salad
   dressing,
more vivid than her bright lipstick.

It's a memory evoked by one word
which, moulded by her Scouse,
enveloped me in an unfamiliar material of maternal
   warmth, comfort and joy.
"Come and give me a *cuddle*!" she'd cry,
as tho' she'd espied a genuine treat.

It's given me a memory
as rich as honey, as warm as the summer sun.

I may weep, as my family, known and unknown,
capsizes into the shadows.
My old aunt has died,
but I have salvaged from
   her a treasure,
in one word,
cuddle.
An everlasting memory,
of love.

A Beautiful Autumnal Day

It is a beautiful autumnal day.
Sky pale blue, like my old aunt's eyes,
leaves gold red, like her hair in her youth;
deliciously fresh and warm,
like my old aunt, whose funeral is today.

My old aunt has died, at 88,
seven months after her husband of 55 years.
Nine months after her younger sister,
her best friend, my mother.
Three sisters have already gone before.

My aunt, who as a child slammed the door on God
and ran away
from an old man with a long beard who'd come to the door.
My aunt, who managed her mother's household of seven children,
who was always out and about, doing and visiting.
Who finessed whatever life threw at her.
What had I done today?
Where had I been?
Her constant questions to me.

LOSS

Having nurtured me as a child,
seen me as an actress born,
she was puzzled by me as an adult:
always at a computer,
working long hours.
I must be earning vast sums of money.
No use explaining I was not.
Her premise was:
life is for living,
not sitting.

A cruel year of bereavement,
crept into her old and lonely bones
and her loving heart, crusting with age,
broke and felled her so she died alone,
in her hallway,
waiting to travel, somewhere,
as it was, into the shadows.

She has gone in the flames
and from her ashes
I wish for the essence of her
to fly into this beautiful autumnal day,
pale blue sky and gold red leaves.
deliciously fresh and warm,
like my beloved aunt, whose funeral was today.

Mimi

You lie in a small grave, under a small headstone.
Your resting place for more than 60 years.
In my childhood, I remember every Sunday, your mother,
my aunt, visited you,
with her three children, my cousins,
the half-sisters and -brother you never knew.
I couldn't understand why
because if you were dead you weren't there.
It seemed so simple.

Aged five. The daughter of my aunt's first husband,
a Polish pilot, shot down and killed in the war.
That's the patch of our inherited backcloth.

I learnt that you'd died of cancer.
That my aunt, married to my father's brother,
was pregnant with the first of her new family,
and couldn't visit you in the London hospital.
But my mother did, bringing you the jam sandwiches
you asked for but couldn't eat.
You died, the day before your half-sister was born.
And all I knew for you was a sorrow thrice over.

I learnt that you were the reason we, who came after,
called my grandmother not Grandma but Auntie Dod.
Because, she'd decreed, you weren't a blood grandchild.
Somehow that decree was handed on to us.
And I was cross with you for that.

I understood little.

Now I visit you, infrequently, and see you alone,
with no family, real or adopted, near you in the graveyard.
And I have no photographs, no memories
of the little girl, my step-cousin, that you were.
But I do have a touch more understanding of why there
   were visits,
every week.
And why your siblings visit
   you now, as your frail
   mother can not.
And for what it's worth, you,
   tho' a stranger, sit in a space
   within me.
And I share this memory
   of you, here, to keep your
   memory alive,
as your frail mother has done
   for more than 60 years.

A Bientôt

Don't think you can leave us that easily.
Your place at the table will be there always—
in the minds of many,
as you will be in our hearts.

It must be hard for you.
But it'll be hard for us, trying to carry on without you
who brighten the march, who lighten the load
in the bleary, early morning trudge to keep fit and play
   the game.

We'll carry on, of course, but
without your ceaseless teasing,
quipping and quaffing, advising
and nurturing us and our kitbag of issues and troubles.

No, don't think you can leave us that easily.
Whoever sits at the table by the lockers,
before the entrance to the gym (you never entered),
will not replace you.
Because you leave the stage,
your presence will not be forgotten.
You have made an impression,
sufficiently deep to ensure
you will live on in our memories,
as well as into the very being of your grandchildren, and
    theirs.

Wherever you are,
in shadows or shine, heaven or hell,
in dust or soil, perhaps on another stage,
with a quiverful of the usual suspect jokes,
I imagine you with a role to play.

So, organise the new place to your liking.
Prepare it for us,
as you hammer hell out of a centre court in the sky.
Assemble the newspapers.
Get the coffee brewing.
Ensure the courts are free, at all times,
for us, your many sports club friends,
who, in time, will follow in your footsteps.
There'll be the old familiar faces:
Tom, teasing and squeezing life out of his old jokes,
Terry the Taxi searching for a seat,
Mike thinking and Maureen bubbling over a new beau,
The Boomer announcing the sporting Georges, I, II and III,
and me, undoubtedly fretting over some new bookbaby
which I'll want you to read rather than use to level up yet another wardrobe.

So, my friend, please, hold on to this thought:
don't think you can leave us that easily.

A Hymn of Hope

O, Lord, in these troubled times,
in the world and in my mind,
let me see a candle light,
let me see it shining bright.
Then ... let me share it.

O, Lord, when I feel alone,
chilled and empty to the bone,
remind me it's the same for everyone,
then let me feel the warmth of the sun.
Then ... let me share it.

O, Lord, when I feel in pain,
racked with troubles and locked in chains,
let me see a bird in flight,
free and spirited, soaring to heights.
Then ... let me share it.

O, Lord, when I come to die,
scared and tired, and wondering why,
let me reach out and touch your hand,
feel in that moment your promised land.
Then ... let me share it.

NATURE

The Old Fox

Quiet as a whisper
the snow has duvet'd the ground,
tog'd it in silence,
and stares back defiantly at the inky, impenetrable night.

It is bitterly cold,
as cold as death
that lurks round every corner,
stalking the unwary creatures of the night.

Quiet as a whisper
the old fox travels along the road
on three stick-thin legs,
the wounded fourth
hovering close to its haunch.

For six weeks or more
the old fox travels different routes,
to and from the neighbourhood,
in search of food
but not followers.

For six weeks or more,
on a thrice-nightly search,
the old fox hobbles through the snow, ice and wind.
Somehow, perhaps in the shadow of his former strength,
he sees off his younger rivals.

Limping he is. Limpy, he's become.
His lush, dense red fur
mange'd in two across his back
by a wide raw band of pink, naked flesh.

He comes close
and closer still for food,
like countless generations of his forebears.
The cat's rejects; our leftovers, a tin of dogfood,
and his daily eggs, which he carries as gently as his cubs.
His eyes are clouded, fatigued, puzzled, sad.
All at once, he reminds me of an uncle, long gone.

Within three days, the leg is no longer lifted
but strong and firm on the ground.

The battle begins between winter and spring,
as it continues between mange and fur.
But I see a break
as,
quiet as a whisper,
the old fox travels through the night and neighbourhood
on four legs.
He is old but such a brave fighter and I hope that, for a
  while,
for the winter, or maybe for the year and beyond,
he has given death the slip.

The Gardener's Boat

A small wooden boat nestles into the thick green foliage;
the water reflects the wood, as well as its secrets,
and holds secrets of its own.

There is a
   stillness,
there is a
   sadness
in the
   air,
in the water
that goes deep, deep
   down
and wide.

Who has been here before
and with a heavy heart,
rowed and towed their tears out into the water?

No one and nothing will tell,
but the trailing leaves
hang heavy with a sorrow
that touches the soul.

Wishful Thinking

You sit there, your striped back to me,
nose at your peak, staring, staring,
up, up and away.

A round red paper spot on a sold picture
and I have captured you – if only for a moment,
if only in an etching.

You remain, in body and spirit, free.
Free to enjoy delights, free to face dangers
and, maybe, to succumb.

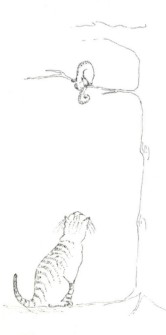

I watch you, staring, staring,
up a tree, to the fidgety
   squirrels;
into the sky, at the autumn
   flights
above us, off into the unknown.
What don't you know that I
   have no need to know?

Once, you fitted into the palm
   of my hand.
Once, you clung to my neck
   with your claws,
as I cling to you now in fear.

What is it that I love and am scared to lose?
Your delicate elegance? Chocolate paws, triangular face,
   tigrous eyes?
The waving tail that flags from side to side in greeting?
Your squeaky call when you come in?
"I am here, where are you?"
Or your independence that takes you off to unknown
   places?

You were lost nearly to maladies unknown,
and a car that damaged your bright brain
but not your spirit.

When you climbed curtains and
turned the household upside down,
I thought you a beast, clawing your way into my life.

Now I see you as a gift, on loan.
To be treasured and kept, 'til you are returned,
please God, way, way overdue.

Then, brave little tiger,
I shall have you in that moment
and only in an etching.
And I shall be staring, staring
and following, following your gaze.
Wondering what it is you never knew
that I have no need to know.

The New Bird in Town

Come, quickly! There's a stranger in town!

A bird the colour of water fern,
a scarlet streak across its head
and the nape of its neck,
is attacking the ground
with the relentless enthusiasm of a pneumatic drill.

A small patch of lawn,
frozen solid by the shock of weeks of snow and ice,
is nevertheless being jackhammered determinedly for live
    food.

This small patch of lawn, where a young rowan tree
    grows,
where a small signpost directs human traffic,
is a dining room (one of many) for the fur'd and feather'd
within our community mix.

Sometimes at night
a badger trudges across it or a fox sits
staring into the bright lights of the houses,
patient and keen for a share of pickings.

The green woodpecker is drilling,
creating a colander of this patch of earth.
It has a penchant for ants and there are many here,
as young boys often find.
The bird's long barb tongue whips into the earth for
a snack, a feast,
and then moves on, swiftly,
the roadbreaking beak given little rest.

The new bird on the block is intent on its business,
apparently oblivious to the regulars.
A blackbird, curious but nervy, hops about,
in a bit, out a bit,
like an L-plated dancer seeking a partner to take to the
    floor.
Two pigeons, which rely on their airbus size to see off
    others,
appear offended: with this intruder, size doesn't matter.

Minutes and many more go by.
The green woodpecker is here for more than one course.
The blackbird and the pigeons fly off
and return, using their same tactics.
But the green woodpecker has its head down,
its beak pointed at the ground.
It is drilling for victory
and nothing and no one is going to interfere.

Welcome, new neighbour.

Mr Turner, I Presume

The man's at it again.
So why am I so surprised
and more enchanted than ever?

He's been at it for more than thirty years,
from before dawn to after dusk.
Ever since I moved in.
And now I'm moving out of this house on the hill
I shall miss him.

There he goes again.
The consummate professional,
never failing to amaze.
Ceaseless.
Soundless.
(Loud noises supplied by others, under his direction,
   I imagine.)

It has to be him, doesn't it?

Who else could work with this vast canvas of sky
stretching from Wembley Arch to Crystal Palace?
Who else could use the rainbow palette
to such magnificent effect?
Who else could create more major works in one moment
than the world's galleries could ever house?
Who could conjure such a magical variance of lights
That makes me weep with joy?
Or evoke drama with shades of darkness?
Who on earth or in heaven could make grey appear
interesting?
Who...?

Hang on, he's at it again.
A fleet of big, buxom clouds move voluptuously across a
bright seaside blue sky.
Look, he's added shimmering tangerine tinges.
He must've met up with that blousy blonde from one of
the TV soaps who's just died.

This man could take your breath away every second of
the day if you yielded to be audience full time.
And, excepting a lull of darkness, here there are no
commercial breaks.

Thank you, Mr Turner.
For thirty years of the privilege of seeing your after-work
   in the after-life.
I can't paint you a glorious thank-you.
I can say only humbly and stumblingly,
I shall miss you more than words can say.

LOVE

Help

You hold out your hand
and I give you mine,
with crumbs of comfort in broken bits of sentences.
They seem so small I wonder if they can nourish or
    sustain.

You look for the way
and I point,
wondering if the signposts
show the right direction.
Will they guide you or lead you astray
into a denser fog?

You need strength
and I build a bridge
out of twigs of succour,
chips of support,
and a mortar of borrowed courage,
wondering if it will endure the storm.

LOVE

You hold out your hand
and I give you mine,
wondering if what passes between us
is snared in a mist of misunderstanding
or drowned in an overwhelming tide of need.

You hold out your hand
and I give you mine,
knowing that they may not touch
and even if they do, that it may not be enough,
while wondering if it's all we'll ever know.

Wedding Blossom

A winter's day, grey as an English pond.
People battling against imperious joint emperors,
wind and rain,
which change their majestic minds, on a whim,
to scatter people this way and that, that way and this.

The room has been sprayed with sunshine.
Yellow freesias and fresh paint
blossoming within four solid old walls,
and from a warm wood base.

In we shuffle, fluffy in our meringue mood,
light as air, sweet-tempered, ethereal,
to celebrate
the happiness and love that is at our heart.

A love not Pimm's but port,
not lace but velvet.
Rich and smooth. Deep as silence.
A good, old-fashioned fire of fresh logs
that warms all who draw close.

LOVE

Two people, whom time, not man, will draw asunder,
stand bereft of coats and umbrellas,
clothed in Sunday best, confetti'd in convention,
and edged with nerves.
A look between, a foot on the firm, familiar bridge
steadies the step, regulates the breath.

There grows an oak.
For the rest, we have an acorn of happiness
to remember on another grey day,
when the light is as dull as stale water.
We can reach into our pockets,
pull out the acorn, and hold and scent,
but for a moment, bright yellow freesias and fresh paint.

Lost Love

I scent you in my heart.
Salt and sea,
smoke and gin,
all eat at the wound
you left.

Though I left you, you're with me still.
I breathe fresh air yet in it are the
strains of you,
refrains of you.
Salt and sea,
smoke and gin.

The soft brush that drew you in me,
that painted the picture I cannot remove
from the wall of my memory,
is now a knife, cutting your image into my soul.
Cold marble filled with blood
that runs from top to toe to find an escape
but there is none. No way out.

LOVE

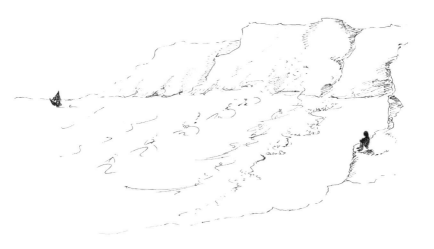

Until I die and turn to marble, inside and out,
then, then, then and then
I can be with you.

Salt and sea,
smoke and gin,
will blow over me
but have no cutting edge.
I shall be one with them and you. Again.

The Love Scavenger

The skater slipped past me, did a figure of eight,
taking me with him, on a short trip.
He half smiled as he let me take his hand
but he did not take mine.

For a brief moment he stood in the light,
although he hungered for shadows.
It was high summer but the skater
sailed secure with the ice beneath his feet.

I knew a long time had passed since he was young,
since a young girl had led him to the edge, to the thaw,
where the ice now roared over the precipice,
in thunderous bolts of tidal life,
lightning flashes of blue and silver,
grey and black,
shooting to the ground.

For the first time, and the last, in the distance,
he'd caught a glimpse of snowdrops, of blossom,
of sunshine, of a life beyond the chilled night.
His eyes were dazzled by the beauty and
he felt a fear of the exquisite pain of ecstasy.

LOVE

Her smile had made him brave.
He'd smiled hearing her laughter
dart in and out of the water.
He went to take her hand, to plunge into the spring . . .
but when he reached out, she had gone.
Her laughter tumbling away from him,
as light as snowflakes in the wind.
A grenade of ice splintered his heart
and a vision was lost on a winter wind.

He returned to live on the ice,
melting only sufficient to ensnare others.
He held me, lightly, at a compelling distance from
  himself.
I was mad to kiss him, and when I did I could taste the
  chill
still on his breath, the frost in his body.
I was mad to inflame his frozen heart,
as he was set on freezing my heat,
when, suddenly, the ice fired a
  thaw on a frozen memory
and I escaped, just –
with a searing bruise within
  my heart –
as I had before.

In Recovery

My heart was bruised when I married.
Another love had caused it to run fast as a cheetah,
soar as high as an eagle.
But a shot, a stumble, a drop,
brought it down. Hard.
To writhe in sorrow and then lie numb in a desert.

My head took command when I married.
Rolling up sleeves, it took control.
Enough of nonsense. No pirouettes of joy.
Passion spent and bankrupted.
Time to dress in harsh logic, no frills of emotion,
put on the heavy winter shoes of common sense,
which crush light spring petals.

Head ruled, while heart lay subservient.
Dormant. Almost dead. Desiccated of feeling.

LOVE

But trickles of days, turn to waves of weeks,
torrents of springs and summers, lead to a heartbeat.
A flutter. Life. Back again.
Learning to walk on unsteady feet,
gaining strength to cut the silhouette
from the abstract picture.

Toddler emotions try again a few
    uneasy steps.
Butterfly crushes crestfallen.
But the heart grows stronger,
holds the head in a gentle
    embrace.
Sense checked, not mated.
Still, the heart can't run
but now it does remember how.

For You

There is a line in the book that's for you.
Only you will know it for what it is,
for what it was, for what it means or meant.

It is all that is left of one summer,
when the coast was our picture window,
and the wind sent clouds
scudding across the top of the frame.

Dried flowers in a vase,
in an apartment dried out from too many people
passing through. Too many lives,
too much sand through the glass.

We threw open the windows,
and brought in fresh flowers.
We picnic'd on the balcony,
we played Scrabble in bed.

We found a crab on the shore,
clicking and clacking,
that reminded us of the old chap
who cleaned our house back home.

LOVE

We clambered over the rocks
and bathed on the beach—
you, so fair, you became a raw filling in a sandwich of *The
 Times*.

We sat in a pocket of sunset, amidst strangers,
eating fish and drinking wine,
gazing, glazing over with love.

We walked in a forest, do you remember?
Sunshine tumbling through the branches
like fish through a net.

I loved you, do you remember?
It's something I won't
 forget, so
the line in the book
 is for you.
It is all that is left
 of that summer,
 that lifetime ago.

Wedding Frost

I stand at your side,
filled with love,
you filling with our child.

Cherry blossom happiness
marred by the knowledge
that the bud is tinged with frost
that a cold hand of winter may well claim,
as I know, my darling, it may claim me.

I shut my eyes to see the sight of you,
without me within you; without me.
The edges of the picture scrape against my eyes,
and bundle my breath into a sob, a knot of grief,
I try to swallow but can not digest.

But I must keep this secret from you,
until I can no longer,
until I am no longer.

Until that day, my darling ...
holding you,
holding back what may or may not come,
I stand at your side,
filled with love.

The Dance

You took my hand and led me to the dance
and your hold reminded me of my father,
who could make a sack of potatoes
look as graceful as silk.

Your touch was lighter,
allowing me to play,
take liberties with the rhythm. And with you.

We quickstepped into marriage
and met one another as strangers
on the other side.

And here we are a decade on,
amidst the scattered roses and thorns,
growing old together.
And possibly, hopefully, wiser.

We have encountered turbulence,
from waltz to tango,
and created for ourselves a Caribbean climate —
with colourful laughter,
amidst the storms and sunshine.

We bring different dishes to the table.
You have brought me courage,
which I've gobbled up greedily,
to pursue my dreams.
You have brought me love and time,
on a platinum tray, listening and guiding.

I wonder what have I brought you?
I hope courage, too,
to explore and fulfil your dreams.
And my greatest gift, after love,
my friends,
a cuddle of extraordinary people:
diverse, talented, different,
adorable people.

So, after all.
Rather a good meal.
Rather a good deal.
Long may the dance
   spin and wheel,
and we continue
   to enjoy the
     mercurial ball.

The Ducks

It's typical of you to find a treasure in a corner.
I must've passed this picture yesterday
but today, with you, I have seen it for the first time.

Here, we stand in a gallery but overlooking a pond,
where in a corner three mallards swim,
the green water rippling outwards.

Trust you, and I do, you see peace
where, in one bird, I see danger.
An attack imminent. A flight.
A war. A death. A sorrow.

I say nothing and you say again, "Yes, here is peace."
For a moment, I glimpse it too.
And silently, not for the first time, I thank you.
And silently, not for the first time, I know why I love you.

FUN

Writer, Beware!

In years long gone,
in town Croydon
there lived a man by name Anon.

Industrious, yet quarrelsome,
he wrote with inspir-a-tion
grim books, dour plays, and serious tomes,
his talents knew no limit-a-tion.

And then all of a sudden, on one fine day
his Muse woke up and moved away.
His pen dried up,
his brain it blanked,
the only job for him was in a bank.

His world gone awry,
he gave a deep sigh,
which was when he found himself slapping his thigh.
He had the answer
and sallied forth
to the city of Liverpool, way up north.

And what do you know?
And what do you think?
No, you're quite wrong,
he did not turn to drink.

FUN

In the land of the Scouse
were people of nous
who taught him to laugh
who taught him to play.
And, in an old-fashioned way,
turned him quite gay.

He donned a red top hat,
he discarded the blues,
sported great tartan boots
and on TV
read the news.

And then, on admission
of a long-held ambition
he decided to become a
   politican.

A good one, too.
So what do you know?
So what do you think?
Did he become another
   so-and-so?

No!
To the people of Liverpool,
he was a real hero!

The Sales

I'm in training for The Sales.
Scrum half; cut back; credit card forward.
And I'm off,
carried on a wave
to save
money.

        I'm in training for The Sales.
        The crush
        the rush,
        the brushing
        against determination
        to get there first.

But where first? Bits of china, chipped glass,
to join the remainder on my shelf.
Shoes too large, too small,
or simply too, too awful.

        Sheets the colour of strawberries long defrosted,
        pillowslips the shade of liquidised peas,
        cheap tickets to sail to queasy, uneasy rest.

Chairs with veneer cracking
beneath the grain,
beneath the strain of it all.
Yes, we're all in training for The Sales.

Inside my old thermal vest, the tension mounts.
And suddenly, in the heat of the (ex-showroom) fitted
   kitchen,
I want out.
                    "I surrender!"
                    But to whom?

I am reduced
to offering myself
at a knockdown (was it the woman with the brolly?) price.
Going cheap. Going anywhere.
As long as it's out.
                        As long as it's off the floor,
                        through the door,
                        and out of the store.
                        Out. Out. Out. Cold.

Price or prize fighter? It's a knockout
and I've hit the bargain floor.
Full price. Fool price. That's me now.
I'm out of training for The Sales.

SPAMutations

He carved in jam,
he sculptured bran,
scenes of life in Twickenham.

But then a trip to old Japan,
a meeting with a courtesan,
the artist was a changèd man.

No longer vegetarian,
and much less a rigid puritan.
No, now a cosmopolitan
and somewhat a comedian.

Thus, a different cupboard love began,
with shows of work that ran and ran,
of erotic sculptures made of Spam.

e-Invitation to a Dance

O, birthday bladerunner
who looked such a stunner
on Saturday night at Wall Hall.

Have consulted the diary, clairvoyant and mind
to enquire when we four are holding a ball
of Lindy-hop – for a birthday blinder.
And now it's over to y'all.

Time's running out
before we head south
(and west),
my flippers, my goggles and me.
Yet
bit time left
(and right) some night
to dance and sip Assam tea.

And then there's you,
off to Peru
with an armful of anti-stuff goo—
to seek Paddington's marmalade mine?
And trews made of lime?
Or other odd things that might rhyme?

So, maybe wait 'til next year
when we could pioneer
another new dance craze or three—
the BladeCrash, the Dolph-Swing, the Garotte, the
   (south) Norwood...?
The list is limit-free.

So, these are my thoughts
and when you pick up this e,
this week or within the next year,
maybe hear from you anon or see you anin
another smoky dance atmosphere.

e-Call to a Friend

O great Naru
where are you?
You have vanish'd from out o' our life.

Is there trouble or strife
in your hectic young life?
Is there anything that I can do?*

Is it teeth that come clatterin',
a'shoutin' and natterin'
and even a flatterin'
you?

Bring us news
or gnus
O great Mr Naru
advisin' us what is the matterin'.

I hope you/yours are well
and, as far as can tell,
think I/we am too, A. Naru.

* I can't paint.

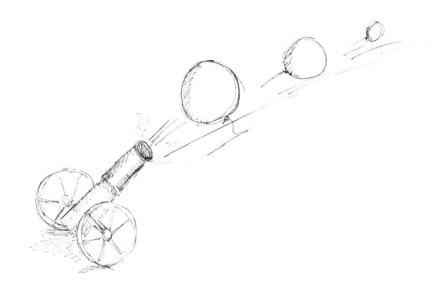

SPLEEN

Farewell to Alms

Let's put aside the life-saving machine,
which is absent from A&E.
Let's not worry that when it arrives its batteries are down
 or out
and that no one has a clue where to find replacements.
That its essential dial is broken
and requires pliers to move but scissors and brute force
 have to do.

Let's put aside the fact a nurse argues with the specialist
who's asked for more fluid when it's obvious to all
but the nurse that the fluid bag is empty.
Let's put aside the skills and compassion of another nurse
 and the specialist,
restoring an elderly woman to smiling good health,
sufficient to leave it to others to carry on her care.

Let's put aside the mask
requiring special plaster that
 has run out
and no one knows where or
 how to get it
and so ordinary plaster is
 used, which
cuts open the ever-watchful
 eye of this feisty old woman.

Let's put aside the time spent calling
for the intensive-care unit over and over again.
Let's put aside the fact that a daughter asks the doctor to
 summon her
from the next room if her mother deteriorates further.
Let's put aside the fact that when the doctor demurs,
she tells him she won't make a fuss:
she was with her father when he died
and she wants to be with her mother.

But her mother dies surrounded by strangers,
with one eye wide open,
the other closed and bloodied
by an unnecessary cut-price procedure.

Let's put aside the weeping young doctor who begs
 forgiveness
when the daughter is called too late to the deathbed.
Let's put aside the hospital operator's repeatedly curt refusal
to give the daughter an outside line to call the undertaker
to take her mother out of this place,
which proves impossible on a Friday night.

Let's put aside the fact that no one explains the cause of death.
Let's put aside the hours spent waiting for someone
to take a dead body to the mortuary.
Yes, let's put aside a life, let's put aside a death.
For in this brave new world of 2009, this is Britain's NHS.

A Year on the Dole
(in the 1990s)

The young woman is on the phone
chatting leisurely in another tongue.
Her long painted nails
push and shove a pile of sweeties
around the desk, within her own orbit.

I sit opposite, silent, sweetless,
feeling similarly pushed and shoved,
and aimless.

She summons an older woman,
mousey curls as tight as her mouth.
She places a reassuring hand on the girl's shoulder
and looks at me, with eyes
the colour and temperature of an English sea in winter.

"Change your career!" she commands,
her voice condescending from an imperious tower.

"I have," I say, although their notes will tell them this.
"I work in PR."
"What's that?" Her voice a few flights higher.

"Public relations,"
    I mutter.
It's hard for a
    journalist to say
    these words,
let alone carry them out, even
    when needs must.

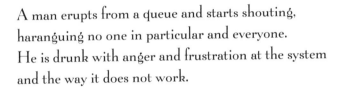

The two women regard me with
    disdain and disbelief.

A man erupts from a queue and starts shouting,
haranguing no one in particular and everyone.
He is drunk with anger and frustration at the system
and the way it does not work.

At home, someone rings the front doorbell,
checking to see if I'm out at work, illegally.
I could be out shopping,
posting more letters seeking work.
The man shrugs and goes away.

I go on an IT course, funded by the government.
There's no teacher and one textbook for a dozen students.
I am reprimanded for photocopying this book
and giving the copies to the eager, desperate students,
before I quit because I'm learning and doing nothing.

Before I quit this centre for time-wasting,
I'm offered a few days' PR work by a kind contact.
As rules demand, I tell the government-funded head of this centre
who asks if he can claim I got the job through him.
No, I say, because you didn't. I got it.

"What's this?" asks my kind contact, waving a letter in the air.
The centre wants my contact to say I got my job through them,
I explain. My contact curses and bins the letter.

(Not many years later, I meet the government's head for this area,
and tell him this story of the funded centre.
He blinks, many times, but says nothing.
More, he does nothing.
The centre continues).

I write letter after letter
and get silence after silence.
Oh, and a handful of (negative) replies.

A man on the tribunal committee calls me a liar.
A reply to a job application, everyone knows, is standard procedure.
His chairwoman intervenes; she knows different now
through her own niece's attempt to get work.
The man shrugs.
The tribunal continues.
The social say I never submitted a necessary form to them,
and then produce the very document I sent in.
But my claim is rejected – because I didn't write enough letters of complaint.

Eventually, I escape the persecution of being told I'm guilty
of not wanting to work, of being branded a liar.
The demeaning humiliation.
The embarrassing fortnightly queue.
I saw cheating. I saw a cranky state-funded system.
And I saw able, capable people go unaided into desperation
courtesy of a failing system aided by small-minded bureaucrats.
I struck lucky. I got a job. I walked free.
I work. Therefore I am – once more.

Daylight Robbery

The lows of a London high street

Live chickens are strangled on the street.
Rats are a supermarket's regulars.
"But they're British Rail rats," the supermarket protests.
No matter. Problem noted and filed. What's next not to sort?

Two young boys slag off a girlfriend,
spraying four-letter words like cheap perfume
or cheaper beer.
No matter. Such performances are regular. By men and women alike.

A man marches along and gobs on the pavement.
No problem. It'll join the rest.

A woman walks past a man
who commands she walk behind him.
No matter. That's life.

A woman in a restaurant talks to the waiter
as if he were a slave.
No matter. He is.

A driver overtakes at speed
a queue of cars in a singled-lane road
to get through the red light.
Not to worry. There are no cameras (surprisingly).

A driver harasses the car in front to go faster
so it's caught by a speed camera.
No matter. The bully isn't caught.

Having barged in front of someone,
a man starts to shout when his lack of manners are
    pointed out, quietly.
He has more important things on his mind, he hollers.
So, that's alright, then.

At lunchtime two men beat up a young girl,
making out she's their slut.
No stranger intervenes.
The police offer her their first free "identity"
  appointment,
two weeks after the event.
She is told to attend a station miles away,
though their HQ is closer to her home.
It's sorted. It's logged. That's enough.

A young assistant in a shop
thanks a customer for saying thank you
because no one else has done so that day.
Or on most others.

We all have our rites
and our rights
to do what we want.
Whenevva.
Whatevva.
It's a "Me first! Screw you!" society.

We are harangued to be "green"
but who decided we throw away please and thank you?
That we attack part of society's mortar?

Who decided to promote respect for self before others?

It's not murder, it's not rape.
It's not racist, sexist, classist.
It is sad(-dist, if you want),
watching the dissolution of manners.
A daylight robbery of times past but not that long ago.

In days of yore, or mine at least,
progress, we were told, was good for us.
And we believed it to be true.
Why doubt those whom we should trust?
But is it progress when
more know less about politesse?

It won't, it can't be a complete or foolproof answer
to this myriad of mess

but

We're destroying the acorns,
the everyday small common courtesies of life,
that grow into oaks
that bind people and communities together,
that help us in our care of one another, and the natural
  world,
more efficiently than cameras,
and in a mightier way than any threat, fine or law can effect.

Author health warning:
adults are advised to enter with a young person.

PLAY AREA

There are Monsters in My Room

There are monsters in my room, said Tania.
And I know why.
They're going to kidnap me
and put me in a pie.

When I wake up in the night
I know that they are there.
They give me such a fright!
They give me such a scare!

You can't see them clearly,
but you know that they are there.
They are made of green goo
and have sticky-out hair.

Some have long fingers,
some have big feet.
You know what they are after.
They're after fresh meat!

MINE!

There's a monster in the cupboard
where I keep my clothes.
He's going to gobble up
all my fingers and my toes.

There's another
in the cupboard
where we keep the towels.
In the middle
of the night
I can hear her yowls.

There's one under the carpet.
There's one under the stairs.
But when Mum and Dad pass by
they completely disappear.

There's one behind the door
that will grin before he grabs you.
There's another in the drawer
that'll chew
right through you.

There's a big hand down the basin
reaching out to strangle me.
And no one will hear me,
however much I scream!

And when I sit on the loo
to do a big poo,
there's a monster there, I know it,
'cos my bottom sees it stare!

One day it will grab me
and drag me under the settee.
It will eat me all up,
belch, burp, fart and—
Hah! Get dreadful hiccups.

(Serve it right!)

My Mum says that there's no one there
and not to be so scared.
My Dad gave me a water spray,
saying, tell them: "Bog off or make my day!"

But I know the monsters,
they just don't care!
I know the monsters
and they are still THERE!

But then one day, Auntie Sue
said, "Listen, Tania,
here's what to do.

"Sing a few bars of your favourite song
and all of those monsters,
well, they'll just sing along.
No one resists
the sound of music,
not even those monsters
who live in your room."

So Tania one night when she went to bed
did exactly, precisely what her old aunt said.
Full of chips, eggs, ham and a dollop of dread
she sang some songs inside her head.

And do you know what?
And do you know why?
Those monsters they danced
'til the sun filled the sky.

They clapped their hands.
They stamped their feet.
To the sound of the music's steady beat.

One, two, three.
One, two three.
Just look and see

The monsters
dancing
so wild and free.

"Oh, Tania," they cried,
horrified
at her fear.
"We're not out to get you,
to brew you,
or stew you.
We simply want to play, my dear.

"To dance and to sing
that is truly our thing.
Please join us, dear Tania,
and get in the swing!"

"Alright," she replied,
and in one, two, three strides,
Tania joined the monsters and danced by their side.

She danced with the monster that lived down the loo.
He was frightfully nice and was made of bamboo.

She danced with the monster that lived under the stairs.
He came from Dundee and had dark tartan hair.

She took tea with the monster that lived in the basin
and found that he kept his Sunday-best face in
a jar of French mustard and iced mandarin.

While the monster who yowled
wore a bright orange cowl,
and brought her a flock of free-ranging fowl.
She had green hair with highlights,
purple and ice white
and, though constantly scowling, was very polite.

They were terribly nice and though great, fat and hairy,
Tania had to admit they were not at all scary.
They fed her iced buns,
helped out with her sums.
She really found them enormous fun.

She's grown up has Tania
and now she tells her
son to sing and to smile
and completely beguile
the monsters that live in his room.

So, remember, my dear,
when the monsters you fear
slip into your bedroom's dark shades,
remember the girl
who sang and who swirled

With the monsters who danced to the day's Hit Parade.
For music can stop you from being afraid
and show that all monsters can be sweet serenaders.

Well, almost all, because there was one ...
But that's another story.

I Want to
Stay Up Late Tonight

I want to stay up late tonight
to watch horror on TV
and eat chips and ham and cold baked beans
and go to bed at three.

I want to stay up late tonight,
I refuse to do seven-thirty.
I don't want a bath. I won't clean my teeth.
I want to stay nice and dirty.

What is the point of going to bed
when I'm not tired, I'm wide awake?
"Turn off the light!"
"You canNOT read!"
No, this is all a big mistake.

Mum yawns, Dad snores in front of the TV.
They should go up the stairs at seven.
Yes, they should go, not me!

Ah...
At last, they've come to bed.

I know what, I'll sneak downstairs,
I'll sneak down in bare feet
now they're in bed
resting their heads
and tucked up between the sheets.

Shh!

I'll turn on the telly
but I'll keep it very,
very,
very
quiet.
Can't wake Mum.
Must not disturb Dad.
Don't want to start a riot.

Yippee! The movie's just starting!
And the vampire is having a party
in a place at the back of beyond.
He's got fangs down to here
which'll cut you like shears.
Mmm. He's certainly no James Bond.

YAWN!

I'm not sure I'll watch this bit.
'Cos he's leaning to kiss
this miss
who's covered in blisters and zits.

YUCK!

O, frogs!
  O, snakes!
  O, heck!
Agh! He's bit right
  through her neck!
Which,
if you want my opinion,
is carrying things to excess.

YOWL!

The girl on the screen looks so frightened.
And there's blood and teeth everywhere.
I'm not sure if I just mightn't
take myself back up the stairs.

But I'm too scared to move,
to turn off TV,
I can't see this through
and I need the loo.

O, what can I do?
I have to poo
and I want to go back to my bed.
I want to crawl under the duvet
and cuddle up to my Ted.

But I can't make it up alone.

O, Mum! O, Dad!
I'd be so glad
if you'd come down to help me upstairs.

And I'll go to bed
it goes unsaid
at whatever time you declare.

Hang on a mo,
before I go,
I'll watch this bit, it looks fun.

The spotty girl's now on the run.
She's escaped and she turns to the camera.
O, my golly and by abracadabra—
She's turned into my MUM!

Overture and Beginners

I'm starting school tomorrow
and I'm as scared as scared can be.
But I'm not telling anybody,
it's a secret between you and me.

I don't want to leave Mum.
I don't want to leave home.
I'm too young to go.
And I'm not full grown.

I'm too small to go into that building.
There are too many big people in there.
They make lots of noise. I can't take my toys.
Not even my special old Bear.

They'll laugh at me at school.
I won't know anyone there.
I want to stay home and curl up
with my Mum in the big armchair.

They'll laugh at me. I know they will.
They'll laugh at my navy-blue knickers.
They'll pull my hair. They'll break my specs.
They'll be trendy and wear brand-new kickers.

They'll be bigger than me. They'll know more.
They'll know where everything is.
I'll get into such a panic.
I'll get into a terrible tizz.

I won't know where the loo is
when I'm desperate for a wee.
And what will I do in the playground
when I fall over and cut my knee?

I won't know anyone to talk to.
No one will know who I am.
What do I do when I'm hungry,
and want some bread and jam?

Or when I want a drink of water
or a great big cup of tea?
There'll be no one there to help me.
There'll be no one who knows ME!

AGH!
I DON'T WANT TO GO TO SCHOOL
   TOMORROW!
WHAT MEANIE MAKES UP ALL THESE RULES?

* * *

It's my first day at school today.
I've got butterflies in my tummy.
It's my first day at school today
and my nose has gone very runny.

Old Bear is deep in Mum's handbag.
Mum's holding on to my hand.
And I've got on a smart new uniform.
But I'm not feeling all that grand.

There's a boy over there and he's crying.
There's a girl who looks kind of glum.
There's a boy with dark hair who looks awfully scared.
There's a girl who is sucking her thumb.

But there is a boy who is grinning.
He is standing all on his own.
"I am so excited," he tells me.
"It's nice not to be alone.

"I've got no brothers or sisters.
My cousins live a long way away.
Will you be my friend?" he asks me.
"Will you play with me, just for today?"

I don't normally talk to boys.
But I said, "Alright. Okay."
And I said to my Mum, "Goodbye, then.
Yep, I think I'll stay for today."

Jake and me we painted.
And then the teacher read.
We played music with spoons
and looked at cartoons
and made strange knotted things with thread.

We had juice and biscuits for brunch.
We ate sausage and chips for lunch.
There is masses to do.
Oh, and I found the loo.
And the other kids are quite a nice bunch.

Mrs Perkins is very friendly.
She smiles a lot and winks.
She takes PE, she reads, she jokes,
she even gets us drinks.

Next week, we all go swimming!
Next month, we visit the zoo!
We'll learn to read
and do lots of sums,
perhaps even lace up my shoes.

I shall see Jake tomorrow.
And Amar, Karen and Rula.
This school thing ain't so bad, really.
In fact, it's almost quite cool. Yeah!

Baby Blues

I've got a new Baby Sister.
She hasn't got a name.
But I tell you, I wouldn't miss her
if she went back from where she came.

She moans all day.
She cries all night.
She's incredibly ugly.
She's a horrible sight.

She's got wobbly legs.
She's got wobbly arms.
She's fat and she's bald.
She has got no charms.

She sicks up her food.
Does loadsa stinky poos.
She smells and farts
and dribbles and can't
do anything to amuse.

She can't play football.
She can't play with me.
And sometimes she's so blotchy
she looks like she's diseased.

She belches and she burps.
She gurgles and she squeaks.
And sometimes she lets out a horrifying SHRIEK!

And everyone goes running
to see what's the matter.
Except for me,
I could just zap her.

She can't stand up.
She can't sit down.
If you ask me, I shall tell you,
she's a pain to have around.

I don't know why they got her.
I don't know what she's for.
I think she's quite useless,
a complete and utter BORE.

Mum thinks she's an angel,
her little bundle of joy.
Puke! How yucky!
I think she's the devil's toy.

When Dad comes home, he rushes in
and tickles her under the chin.
He picks her up. He cuddles her.
I think he likes her better.
But little do Mum and Dad know,
I am going to get her.

I used to be their favourite.
I used to be Number One.
When it was Mum and Dad and me
we had oodles and bundles of fun.

But now they shout and scream at me:
Keep Quiet! Don't do that!
Keep AWAY!
You'll wake the Baby!
You'll make her cry!
But still I disobey.

Who cares? I want to shout.
Get rid of her! Kick her out!
I want it like it used to be,
us three:
Mum,
Dad
and me!

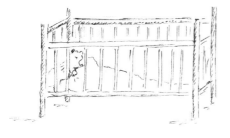

Mum says I'd miss her,
my Baby Sister.
But she doesn't know
hi-di-hi-di-hi-ho!
How I'd like to kiss her
GOODBYE!

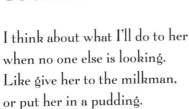

I think about what I'll do to her
when no one else is looking.
Like give her to the milkman,
or put her in a pudding.

Or put her in the garden shed
or cover up her head
with ice cream, liquorice, and cold baked beans
and leave her 'til she's dead.

I hate her. I hate her. I hate her.
I hate her with all of my might.
I HATE HER SO MUCH it scares me.
It really gives me a fright.

Then one night I dreamt I'd killed her,
got rid of her, once and for all.
I woke up in a real cold sweat.
And
then
I
heard
her
SQUAWL!

I crept into her bedroom.
I looked into her cot.
She was crying fit to burst
and her nose was covered with snot.

She looked up and she saw me
and gave me such a grin.
She gurgled and laughed and waved her arms
as if to say, "That's HIM!

"That boy's my great Big Brother!
He's big and strong! Take care!
He's my hero.
He can do anything! So you there—BEWARE!

"He climbs up trees.
He can (almost) read.
He's as wonderful as can be!
And I'm so very proud of him,
'cos he is the Brother of Me!"

'Course, she didn't say all of that really.
It just looked like she did to me.
I suppose she's not bad,
I told Mum and Dad,
when they came into the room.

She's alright,
sort of,
this yucky bundle of joy.
Though I have to say,
whatever they claim,
she'll never be as good as a boy.

But hang on.
What if she's better . . .?

HAPPY ENDING

The Face Rainbow

You can't eat it but you can drink it in.
You don't need special ingredients to make one
or spend hours in the kitchen preparing it.
You'll find them in clubs and cafés, on tap but not bottled,
and at 'most any place on earth.

You don't have to sign up for one.
Sit down or stand up to acknowledge one.
You don't have to be accompanied by an adult to try one
   out.
You don't have to be accompanied at all.
And you can't be underage.

You don't have to loiter at a bus stop in the pouring rain
before one comes along.
You don't have to trawl the internet
or sail the seven seas
in search of one.
Oh, and there aren't special offers, or 3 for 2,
in any supermarket or bookshop.

You don't have to take classes to learn how to create one.
You don't have to get dirty, or remain spotlessly clean,
or buy special clothes or expensive trainers
to help you put one into action.

HAPPY ENDING

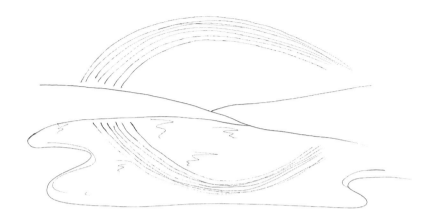

You don't have to save up for one.
Rich or poor,
anyone can wear one.
Chances are it'll suit them all
and give them a special glow.

It doesn't come from anywhere defined,
except perhaps, and loosely, your heart.
It costs nothing to give, nothing to receive.

It's free.
No down payment.
No final demands.
No hidden extras.
No small print.
No hidden agenda.

You can invest in millions
and it won't bankrupt you.
It might even pay you dividends beyond your wildest
 dreams.

Give one – it's free, remember –
perhaps to a passing stranger,
and with luck, and again at no cost,
you get one back.

And then you'll both pass by lighter footed,
with a touch of fresh sunshine inside
and the shimmering brilliance of that fleeting rainbow.

You can't buy it,
and what it contains,
but you can drink it in.
And share it around.

What is it?
    It's a
        smile.

Information Area
If you want to know how a poem in this book came into being, enter here. If not, leave immediately.

LOSS (p.11)

The Time Chasm (p.12)
A small table stands between us but it is two hands that divide us
For Lord Cottesloe, Deputy President of the National Rifle Association, at the time I was researching and writing its history, *The Queen's Prize*. He was an erudite, dry-humoured and dignified gentleman who kindly read the proofs of the book. It was a joy to be in his company.

One of the Good People has Gone (p.14)
One of the good people has gone
For the wife and daughters of John, a dear unassuming man who died suddenly and unexpectedly, and too young.

Becalmed Within a Storm (On the loss of a close friend) (p.16)
An autumn sun shines benignly
For John's sporting friends.

The Visitor (p.20)
She'd never noticed the visitor before
If you're wondering, I've not succeeded – the poem is about death.

My Old Aunt has Died (p.24)
My old aunt has died
My uncle asked me to say something at my aunt's funeral and, again, poetry came easier than prose. I wanted to write down what little I knew of the colourful life that my aunt, my mother and my forebears had led.

A Beautiful Autumnal Day (p.28)
It is a beautiful autumnal day
The day of my aunt's funeral reminded me much of her strong, bright personality.

Mimi (p.30)
You lie in a small grave, under a small headstone
For a fatherless little girl who died too young.

A Bientôt (p.32)
Don't think you can leave us that easily
For Tony, who, aside from his games of tennis, has sat at the same table in the sports club for more years than most members can recall, teasing and entertaining everyone who passes by. And somehow attracting 'most everyone to sit down and join him.

A Hymn of Hope (p.35)
O, Lord, in these troubled times
I rather like singing hymns. So one day I decided to write one.

NATURE (p.37)

The Old Fox (p.38)
Quiet as a whisper
Our street has had foxes for years. I like to think that Limpy is the great-great-etc-grandson of a gentle vixen that used to chill out happily in the sunshine on the flat roofs of the garages alongside my otherwise timid little cat.

The Gardener's Boat (p.41)
A small wooden boat nestles into the thick green foliage
Inspired by a painting I bought at an exhibition of work by (fantastic) local artists, I thought an Ophelia might have passed this way.

Wishful Thinking (p.42)
You sit there, your striped back to me
For a beloved mini-tiger.

The New Bird in Town (p.44)
Come, quickly! There's a stranger in town
For the beautiful green woodpecker that came drilling for victory.

Mr Turner, I Presume (p.47)
The man's at it again
For the artist in the sky.

L O V E (p.51)

Help (p.52)
You hold out your hand
I wrote this for a friend going through a bad patch. Perhaps it could also apply to a poet reaching out to a reader.

Wedding Blossom (p.54)
A winter's day, grey as an English pond
When I arrived at the wedding of two adorable friends they thrust a camera into my hands. Because I was a journalist, they said, I was to be the official photographer. On such an occasion, one doesn't argue. Come to think of it, I can't recall ever seeing the results. But some time later I did get a gorgeous godson.

Lost Love (p.56)
I scent you in my heart
Separation doesn't necessarily stop love or erase memories.

The Love Scavenger (p.58)
The skater slipped past me, did a figure of eight
Love's magnetic web.

In Recovery (p.60)
My heart was bruised when I married
Love is a many-splinter'd thing.

For You (p.62)
There is a line in the book that's for you
Memories.

Wedding Frost (p.64)
I stand at your side
A lovely wedding, an adoring couple, and an age gap.

The Dance (p.65)
You took my hand and led me to the dance
For I.D.E.

The Ducks (p.67)
It's typical of you to find a treasure in a corner
This is for my friend Pat who bought this picture at an exhibition we visited.

FUN (p.69)

Writer, Beware! (p.70)
In years long gone
Perhaps because it's harboured a number of my relatives, including my mother, I have a great fondness for Liverpool. And it sticks in my mind that, years ago, I interviewed a theatre director, a southerner returning home to London, who was exhausted (happily) because most every Scouser was a comedian.

The Sales (p.72)
I'm in training for The Sales
Written for a friend.

SPAMutations (p.74)
He carved in jam
Written long ago when I had fond memories of Spam, burnt chips and tomato ketchup.

Why can't emails be poetry?

e-Invitation to a Dance (p.75)
O, birthday blade-runner
Written for three dancing friends and bladers, one of whom became my husband.

e-Call to a Friend (p.77)
O, great Naru
Written to Amar, a dentist and a multi-talented star, who goes off radar for long periods.

SPLEEN (p.79)

Farewell to Alms (p.80)
Let's put aside the life-saving machine
This is how my mother died. I wrote a letter to the hospital and their reply implied that I wasn't to worry because any mistakes were being sorted.

A Year on the Dole (in the 1990s) (p.82)
The young woman is on the phone
Being on, or off, the dole, is difficult enough so I think it's something that ought to be experienced long term by those implementing "helpful" procedures. (2010: The mother of a long-term unemployed youngster read this poem and said little has changed.)

Daylight Robbery (p.86)
Live chickens are strangled on the street
As spoken by me and the Greek chorus here in south London.

PLAY AREA (p.91)

There are Monsters in My Room (p.92)
There are monsters in my room, said Tania
A friend's young daughter was frightened of going upstairs and I wrote this to console her. I don't think I did a very good job but it did set me off writing verse for the very young.

I Want to Stay Up Late Tonight (p.99)
I want to stay up late tonight
As a child, hearing TV at a distance can be compellingly attractive. Add laughter or dramatic music . . .

Overture and Beginners (p.103)
I'm starting school tomorrow
I was lucky. I was so excited to start school that, on my first day, I couldn't understand why so many children were crying. Wisely, my mother said she had no idea either.

Baby Blues (p.108)
I've got a new Baby Sister
And I so wanted a big brother.

HAPPY ENDING (p.115)

The Face Rainbow (p.116)
You can't eat it but you can drink it in
Someone replied to an email, thanking me for making her smile. It made me think.